GREEN LIVING 2.0

GREEN LIVING 2.0

FIONA STERLING

CONTENTS

1. Introduction to Green Living 2.0 — 1
2. Energy Efficiency in the Home — 3
3. Sustainable Transportation — 5
4. Green Building Practices — 9
5. Waste Reduction and Recycling — 13
6. Water Conservation Techniques — 15
7. Sustainable Food Choices — 19
8. Community Engagement and Advocacy — 23
9. The Role of Technology in Sustainability — 25
10. Corporate Sustainability Initiatives — 29
11. Government Policies and Regulations — 31
12. Educational Programs and Resources — 33
13. Case Studies in Sustainable Living — 35
14. Measuring and Tracking Sustainability Goals — 39
15. The Future of Green Living — 41

Copyright © 2024 by Fiona Sterling
All rights reserved. No part of this book may be reproduced in any manner whatsoever without written permission except in the case of brief quotations embodied in critical articles and reviews.
First Printing, 2024

CHAPTER 1

Introduction to Green Living 2.0

As the online buzz about green living grows into a crescendo, people are becoming increasingly aware of the need for change. Our purchasing choices and the manner in which we live today affect our future. Still, old sustainable living manuals, which date decades, if not centuries, back, often fall short in providing us with suitable solutions for the world we live in today. Hence, it is time to upgrade the concept into Green Living 2.0: a forward-thinking philosophy grounded in practical solutions for a sustainable future.

Green Living 2.0 is designed to apply to all segments of modern society. Its focus, however, will be on residential, commercial, and professional opportunities, as these are possibly the least understood subjects by the general public. Key areas under consideration include energy, materials, water, waste, and lifestyle. Green Living 2.0 emphasizes three principles - reduction, efficiency, and ecological impact - which form the foundation of sustainable lifestyles today. Promoting a connected, integrated approach, it places equal emphasis on small, simple measures that the vast majority can adopt and larger, profound strategies that others will develop and use. This 'big picture-small picture' approach is designed to reach a diverse global audience at various levels of awareness and motivation.

Understanding the Importance of Sustainability

In this chapter, we show that the long-term wellbeing of society, the economy, and individual companies depends upon a sustainable approach to economic development. We are not advocating that the government should attempt to micromanage these outcomes. This has been proven to be impractical. Economic development is better managed by the private sector. Our responsibility, as citizens and businesspeople, is to ensure that the general framework of laws, taxes, and regulations encourages the private sector to take a sustainable approach to developing the economy.

The health of our planet is the essential underpinning of our economy and our lives. This is the reason why a book about business and personal leadership might devote the first two chapters to a compelling topic such as sustainability. We must do this because without a reasonably healthy and functioning planet, little else matters. Sustainable human development is essential to business because it provides a competitively superior context for the enterprise, the primary economic institution of our society. A sustainable world economy is a precondition for global peace, for poverty elimination, and for the preservation of the environment.

CHAPTER 2

Energy Efficiency in the Home

The most important steps should be vested in improved integration of new technologies into smart design. Without increased emphasis here, it will be impractical to expect significant reductions in energy waste and greenhouse gas emissions. As energy costs increase and alternative energy sources mature, it will become increasingly easier for individuals and businesses to meet energy demand by purchasing energy produced from decentralized sources. However, for this scenario to develop, there needs to be a new energy delivery and management model. This model should be comprised of a two-way network that communicates with a distributed electricity generation/storage device. It could be comprised of an interconnection of everyday items such as water heaters, air conditioners, washing machines, and electric cars.

The first place to start is by embracing energy efficiency in the home. Increasing the efficiency in our energy usage at home is the most cost-effective way to minimize greenhouse gas emissions and make us less susceptible to significant swings in energy prices. Government and business need to assist energy efficiency by investing in a variety of new technologies and by providing incentives for home and business owners to do the same. These include offering: tax credits for the purchase of energy efficient appliances, heating and cooling systems; rebates for energy efficient purchases; deductions for the use of solar and wind systems; and reduced loan rates for the purchase and installation of energy efficient systems in new and existing housing.

Renewable Energy Sources

Today, more and more homes, offices, and factories are using clean energy sources to produce electricity for their own needs—this is called distributed energy and it is an important part of smart grid technologies. Although distributed technology is expensive to set up and may not always produce as much electricity as traditional power plants, the benefits make it a viable business solution. As noted, the benefits of using renewable distributed energy sources outweigh the liabilities. Small-scale solar-powered equipment is also available to individual homeowners who may wish to use the energy produced to heat water, warm their houses, or lower the cost of their electricity bill. With clean renewable energy, even "degree days" won't give consumers the chills!

Renewable energy sources, unlike coal, oil, natural gas, and uranium, are used to create electricity that generates no harmful emissions. Instead, clean energy sources renew themselves—these include geothermal, biomass, wind, water, and solar energy. By using clean renewable energy sources like these, we can protect our environment and keep poisons like radioactive wastes out of our atmosphere.

CHAPTER 3

Sustainable Transportation

We must refocus our transportation investments away from outdated, car-dependent sprawl towards options that can serve everyone. We need transportation facilities that allow people to get around without cars: better bicycle and pedestrian infrastructure, as well as high-quality mass transit. We also need to make it easier for people to live closer to the places they need to go, such as shopping and workplaces. Fossil fuels emit nearly 2.5 million pounds of dangerous pollutants into the air each day. In contrast, electric vehicles loaded with renewable energy release almost no pollution. So shifting away from oil and towards sustainable energy can solve the oil and air quality crises in one package.

With the recent spike in oil prices, transportation has become a frequent topic in the news. And for good reason: Americans no longer have the option of ignoring the exorbitant costs of our car culture. In recent years, U.S. greenhouse gas emissions have been growing fastest in the transportation sector, and car-related air pollution contributes to 30,000 premature deaths every year. The good news is that we can fix these problems by making smarter choices: driving less, using more fuel-efficient vehicles, and fueling them with low-carbon renewable energy. Designing communities to facilitate walking, bicycling, and mass transit will make our transport systems more efficient, ultimately saving time and money while improving health at the same time.

Electric Vehicles and Public Transport

Mass transit can mean taking the bus, taking the train, taking BART, or even using ride sharing programs. Public transport is one of the most affordable ways to mitigate climate change. It reduces oil usage, reduces the number of cars on the road, making everyone else's commute quicker. In congestion delays, puts different cities closer together, opening more job opportunities to those with no car. The inconvenience of having no car is offset by the lower cost of housing, which can result in a dramatically better lifestyle in a place where a car is less needed and transit is an option. Grist has looked at various lifestyle choices with the objective of reducing carbon emissions, comparing the impact of different actions. They identified the best choices, taking into account both impact and convenience. They found that not having a car by itself reduces the impact of a family to the EPA's ultimate goal.

Other options focus on plug-in hybrids; the idea is to have electric cars for short trips and a small gasoline engine for longer trips. These cars can also be more efficient because the engine does not need to run in a low load. The advantages of this fuel diversity spans across industries: we already have a good gasoline infrastructure; electricity grid improvements can be more gradual.

Electric cars are one of the most promising ways to reduce our dependence on oil and to mitigate climate change. However, an electric car is just as green as the source of the electricity it is getting. Most grids are heavy on fossil fuels, which creates a classic of the chicken versus the egg. If no renewable or nuclear power is available, then chances are you are not helping the environment when you plug in your car.

CHAPTER 4

Green Building Practices

To date, the focus has been mainly on sustaining a healthy planet by designing more sustainable buildings, where the aesthetic, social, and economic success of urban or rural communities are being considered. The old aesthetic paradigms of beautiful and lasting forms will continue to endure. Meanwhile, from the philosophical, practical, and commercial points of view, the trend to make more efficient and livable buildings can be emphasized. Only if we know the paths that we already have at our disposal can we be able to choose a better one for our future. There is a reason that the bird in the hand was worth enshrining; make good use of what is already possible, and make the world a better place for the present and future generations.

The way in which our society designs, constructs, and maintains the architecture and infrastructure has significant environmental impacts. However, environmentally responsible design and engineering have made great strides in the past two decades, improving the way of life while attempting to minimize the need for constant human maintenance and resource drain. This essay describes some of the "Green Building" practices and designs that can reduce and help us put our architecture and infrastructure in sustainable development goals. From compact development to urban heat islands and green roofs, to low-energy buildings and sustainable communities, to the increase in use of renewable materials and construction with minimally invasive means, there are no shortages of things that can be done to help us make a change to the presently unsustainable path.

LEED Certification and Sustainable Materials

The Leadership in Energy and Environmental Design (LEED) certification process has become the premier standard in measuring the success and effectiveness of a green building. Since its inception, the US Green Building Council has registered and certified over 1721 projects, providing abundant market evidence of the demand for such buildings. The Energy Star program, which is a joint venture of the US Environmental Protection Agency and Department of Energy, has been adopted by the UK, through the Carbon Trust, as an independent validation of one-sixth of UK landlords' claims to greenness. In response to an increasing demand for a UK rating system, the various chapters of the Royal Institute of Chartered Surveyors are developing the RICS Sustainability assessment of a building design. In addition, South Africa now has its own Green Building Council, while others are under development in New Zealand and Australia. Many rating, certification, and professional organizations have appeared worldwide in response to the tremendous consumer demand for feedback on the environmental performance of building projects. In the United States, many states have considered or passed legislation that effectively mandates the construction of green, sustainable, or energy-efficient buildings to LEED standards. With varying levels of support and enforcement, these legislative initiatives typically establish guidelines and possibly funding for state-funded building projects.

The construction and operation of buildings have a profound positive or negative impact on both our natural and built environment. Many people, when presented with the idea that a building can be constructed or operated in a manner that preserves precious resources and greatly reduces or eliminates the environmental impacts, are interested in the concept and wish to incorporate sustainability into their projects as much as possible. This attitude has recently blossomed into a stellar consumer demand for green, eco-friendly buildings. Green residential buildings have been shown to have some 20% to 31% increases in selling price discounting locational and other factors. Green commercial buildings have been reported to earn 3% to 8% in increased rents and 6% to 18% in cap rates. Leach and Borrmann illustrate this demand by stating that, given the choice, over 80% of households are willing to pay 5% to 10% more for energy-efficient or better comfort in indoor climate. In order to assist designers, owners, and occupants in reconciling all possible needs in realizing a finished green building, standards for measuring greenness have been established.

CHAPTER 5

Waste Reduction and Recycling

Resource recovery centers could sort, process, repurpose, and store materials. Every person would eventually work on a specific task, fulfilling their natural talent and abilities. If products are too difficult to process on an industrial scale, sorted materials could be sent to a central location to serve as a seed charge to encourage local manufacturing and repurpose businesses or regional bio-refineries and other production facilities located near source collection areas. Other waste management approaches that optimize resource efficiencies may require a multi-element solution that is applied in certain locations with specific economic, technological, and labor development capabilities. The side benefits of implementing waste management programs create a tremendous quality of life while solving local and global environmental and waste disposal challenges.

Sustainable and clean living would not be possible without creating systems that maximize resource efficiency, minimize pollution generation, and promote local and circular economies. A door-to-door resource recovery collection system would facilitate waste separation and reduction for disposal products, organic materials, large bulky items, and other recyclables. These materials could then be processed at resource recovery centers, maintaining or creating as many local jobs as possible. Jobs could be created to design, manufacture, operate, maintain, and service products and systems at resource recovery centers and collection services.

Composting and Upcycling

In nature, organic material moves naturally through the cycle of life and death during the process of decay, and composting introduces just the right conditions (water, oxygen, and a little bit of food to feed the detrivores) to keep this cycle bust, even in a pile of kitchen scraps and leaves. This pile that you create is a rich community of microorganisms, insects, and fungi, which keep busy breaking down the already broken down material even further into pieces small enough to incorporate into the soil. In addition to avoiding the methane gas that results from anaerobic decay of organic waste in the landfill, properly composted material reintroduces carbon into the soil and can also positively influence water retention and the availability of nutrients for plants grown in the soil.

A simple, inexpensive, and efficient way to reduce landfill waste while creating a valuable addition to your home garden is to compost. Organic waste - fruit and vegetable scraps, bread, coffee grounds, leaves, and grass clippings - comprises close to 20% of our total household waste. When we send this waste to the landfill, we miss the opportunity to profit from the decomposing organic garbage, namely in the opportunity to reduce our carbon footprint and also to create an incredibly rich soil additive. Composting is also a great opportunity to make the very circular practice of upcycling, or creatively repurposing what would otherwise be waste to some beneficial use, a part of your daily practice.

CHAPTER 6

Water Conservation Techniques

One way around the problem is by using a bucket to collect hot water as the water is drawn, collecting all of the piping cool frequently. If the water is collected, collecting a quart (or more) can ensure that excess piping cool is removed and you receive hot water when the bucket is used for collecting hot water. The bucket is 3 gallons, so once filled it will release the water pretty quickly. If a bath or longer shower is in the offing, you may keep the cool fresh water in the bucket at the bucket while the heating system runs so that you are able to collect your piping cool, effectively utilizing your recirculating hot water piping system and saving some water some of the time. Of course, the best solution is to obtain positive returns in green technologies so that the initial investment can make money over time. Recirculating hot water pumps are excellent options.

This system has a pipe connected to the end of the storage tank that taps off hot water, the one used for showers, sinks, and other applications it is close to. Normally, once water is heated, it simply sits in the storage tank, waiting to be used the next time. An obvious problem with recirculating piping is the loss of hot water from the pipes as it cools, which will cool your water pipes when you use hot water. Since cold shower or sink water is available when no hot water is present, in a typical scenario, when you turn off the tap, you return cooling liquid to the once hot water tank that has been heating water all day – not a good situation for water storage.

After considering the considerable cost of paying for water, many people may feel ready to install an expensive tankless or tanked on-demand water heater and a water recycling system like those used in new houses or even spend $6,000 to install a portable hot water recirculating pump system to save the stored water that drains as you wait for the hot water to arrive. While it is certainly possible to save a lot of water and money by taking such measures, getting there may be challenging. However, one very simple thing to do that costs nothing involves the effective use of the traditional hot water recirculating system, albeit a little unconventional in nature.

Rainwater Harvesting and Greywater Systems

With some of the nation's water resources in California, state regulators have recently issued preliminary building and plumbing guidelines that could also help municipalities meet the state's efforts to reduce greenhouse gas emissions. Called graywater, this "untapped" source of water (already used for irrigation in the poorest nations) accounts for about 50-80% of indoor water in a typical home. In arid lands where most water consumption occurs, the initial payback time is one to five years. Additional benefits are found in improved conservation levels and indoor air quality, as well as value in promoting local well-being and "planning for Catalina Island's sustainable future".

One of the many hidden costs of increasing urbanization is the excessive presence of impervious features - those construction materials that cause water to run off the land rather than be absorbed into it. This is also a leading cause of polluted waterways. Rainwater harvesting combines simple technology with a water-saving technique that can be practiced by nearly everyone. Using rainwater for irrigation and other applications not requiring portable (drinkable) water can offset over 50% of indoor outflow from a typical home. Greywater systems, a newer technology making serious urban inroads, recycle a large portion of what would otherwise head to treatment centers. Even the high cost of many systems is minimal once annual savings in utility bills. Other benefits include the mitigation of expensive infrastructure problems, decreased air pollution, less lawn destruction, and decreased insect infestation. With increasing residential water restrictions and water pollution, the practice is being more widely (and legally) accepted, although some communities are still working towards local policies.

CHAPTER 7

Sustainable Food Choices

Today, well over half of us live in cities, where supporting local food production is much more challenging. That being said: There are still lots of ways urban dwellers can support local foods – even those of us without a farmers market nearby. First and foremost – cook at home. Despite evolving trends, grocery stores still provide limited food choices when compared to a well-stocked kitchen. Fortunately, communities are joining together to create convenient (and affordable!) alternatives. Consider joining a Community Supported Agriculture (CSA) program. Every week, these programs drop off a selection of seasonal produce at a convenient location in your neighborhood. While the options can be overwhelming, it's a fantastic way to become a more discerning shopper. Not interested in a CSA? Look for locally grown produce with the Eco-label of the farmer's market right in your grocery store – some large chains are beginning to source local produce.

One easy way to reduce our environmental impact is by eating lower on the food chain. Plant foods - fruits, veggies, grains, legumes, etc. - are generally much more efficient and sustainable to produce than animal foods. In fact, the average meat-eater is responsible for almost twice as many greenhouse gas emissions as a strict vegetarian. Yet despite the known benefits of eating less meat and dairy, our consumption of animal foods is on the rise. Fortunately, there's no need to go vegan overnight – just start with a "No Meat Monday", or try eating plant-based meals for breakfast, lunch, and/or snacks. Another simple way to change your eating habits? Eat in tune with the seasons. Eating seasonally is good for the environment (it supports and preserves local farmlands), our wallets (in-season foods are much cheaper), and our taste buds (vegetable flavors are most intensively bright during the season when they're meant to be eaten). Summertime means fresh berries, tomatoes, and stone fruit. As the weather cools, apples, pears, and pomegranates move into our farmers markets. In winter-time, root vegetables and squash are at their peak. Greens become in-season in early spring, followed by strawberries in late spring. This year, celebrate the season by trying a new fruit or vegetable every week.

Plant-Based Diets and Locally Sourced Produce

If you're looking for an area in which there's lots of low-hanging fruit when it comes to being green, eating locally probably leads the list. After all, farmland is the largest single man-made change in New Hampshire and most of the northeastern United States. Yet we make surprisingly little use of it. For example, as I have shown above (a few paragraphs and a photo) it is in fact the case that one of New Hampshire's most defining features – its rolling, rock-ridden fields – are being converted in favor of a much less aesthetically pleasing monocrop. But the problem with monocultures isn't just that they look bad; the real trouble is that they are fundamentally unhealthy. They're unhealthy because they tend to be disease magnets (note that tomatoes in a community garden are healthier than those isolated on a farm) and because they require enormous and unnatural energy inputs to maintain. And on the customer end, they aren't healthy either, because they tend to show up in ready-made, highly processed meals.

It should be little or no surprise that one of the single most effective ways to improve both your personal health and that of the planet at the same time is simply to stop eating meat and other animal products. While the notion of individual vegetarianism has likely been around for as long as human civilization has, large-scale vegetarianism as a phenomenon has typically had more to do with observant religion than anything. Claire and I are not religious in the least, so it wasn't any religious group that would persuade us to abandon meat and dairy products – especially since, to be perfectly honest, the religious types I'm most familiar with aren't particularly interested in helping animals or the environment.

CHAPTER 8

Community Engagement and Advocacy

Mandating responsibility for products and practices is a continuing, effective tactic that can take the sustainable agenda a step further. Ten years ago, The Natural Step presented a systematic basis for defining what is ecologically acceptable, and one of the principles it enunciated has been captured in the idea that a producer should be responsible for a product "from creation to grave." This tenet can be expanded and supported both legally and through community initiatives to include the marketing impact of products as a sphere of responsibility. Such discussions are continually unfolding in industry and the general press, but wherever possible, they may need to be supported to bring about long-term change.

While corporations and governments have a crucial role in the development of sustainable products and practices, there is also much that citizens can do to speed up the transformation to a less waste-intensive, more energy efficient, more equitable, and more compelling society. In the context of our consumer-oriented society, businesses cannot ignore the practical solutions put forth by its citizen consumers. As one of the largest investors in the stock markets as well as property, citizen consumers continue to exercise significant influence over these elements of the economy. As there are a wide variety of everyday actions that have a significant current impact, they can be important channels for identifying and tackling the long-term concerns.

Volunteer Opportunities and Grassroots Movements

There are also many organizations and movements which, although they are active and influential, do not even have websites (which is a bad idea for most organizations, except in the sense that more people should have access to computers to read them – not less). Some of these grassroots movements often coincidentally pass by unnoticed on their way to success. Magazines such as Yes! or Orion are good sources to check for opportunities, as well as for bringing news of other great little-known NGOs and community endeavors to your attention in the first place.

I hope that much of the information and the contact resources in Green Living 2.0 are useful to you. Just so you can get out and take action right away, here are a few places where your help may be needed. There are many other guides for other cities available from volunteer centers in other regions of the country. You may find them through United Way offices or by calling 411 directory assistance, an online search, or visiting. In addition to the United Way, other organizations listed in this section such as Volunteer Match, Network for Good, and the Student Conservation Association will help match you with the right organization with a cause you care about, perhaps through their websites.

CHAPTER 9

The Role of Technology in Sustainability

Second, the extra organic information managed by workflows structured for accountability facilitates that by focusing attention on the world outside the organization, on promises made by the organization. Such a record is likely to capture community attention more than smaller snippets of information linked to individual workflows, just because it is the sum of all the parts due to related concrete actions. If I commit to turn off the lights, air conditioning, and computer at work one night before I leave, another time we agreed in one room during a meeting, etc., my entire commitment is neatly encapsulated in one measurable quantity, one specific action. The record also provides for the organizational learning needed to improve its own local behavior. Without such a local learning component, the institutional shareholders of the legal entity are not behaving in the sense described by the HR model.

First, practical clues for developing IT solutions specifically geared towards sustainability can be abstracted from the three forms of information: financial measurements for accountability, natural languages for group discussion, and performance indicators for policy-making. Its central argument is that other community-based metadata vocabularies exist for many activities typically conducted in structured e-Workflows. Existing consensus standards and ongoing collaborative vocabulary projects make it possible to extend workflows so that they lend themselves to accountability. Such workflows will provide a record of real work on sustainability actions, and monitoring of that work as described in this chapter will provide the record and also assignments that may be used to tally the original commitment.

The last chapter argued for the triple bottom line as a model for business organization and suggested that information technology can help businesses organize according to this model. This chapter goes further by examining how information technology can help the community as a whole move toward the triple bottom line. This chapter includes ideas for businesses, technology developers, and society itself.

Smart Home Devices and Energy Monitoring

One obvious, and yet catchy, solution to turning off lights or plugging into a power strip our home office and bedroom appliances is to manage such devices remotely. Occupancy sensors, the descendants of an estimated 200-mask artist, report back to Alexa, who makes life more convenient and also shares energy monitoring graphs on the Web. In addition, smart devices can help utilities reduce demand at peak times, or smart meters such as SmartSynch may also be used in the future to analyze spatial and temporal energy use patterns at a much finer resolution. What graphical practice may emerge at a next-level in the residential game? Currently, the proof is quite literally in the power savings. At least superficially, much of the fluff has been whittled away in the $99-across-the-board range of devices currently selling on the market. Notably, (nearly. there's always exceptions) the bad rap that device manufacturers get when developing "energy-efficient" devices has hurt their sales, as consumers recognize that features lose some appeal at the expense of power. And so, now, we have a second wave. The feature-rich time has come to enchant the consumer once again, only this time in a much more intelligent, and serious, way. Enjoy your seconds, again and again, and turn your lights off tomorrow night. Keep your home investment intact and the cost of electricity down. These are good things. I like good things. What about you?

I don't know about you, but my mother had a sixth sense when it came to knowing whether or not you'd turned off the lights. She wouldn't let you leave the house unless you'd walked into each room for a short check of the guest room and the upstairs hallway for good measure. For as simple as it would seem today to install motion-activated lights or programmable lighting, power-conscious controls have just recently come onto the market at a reasonable cost. Beyond lights, a slew of electronic devices offers enormous power savings during their off-hours. Although we'd like an LCD TV, a cable box, and speakers to act like the near-future "end" button on our computers, these devices, more often than not, continue to draw power long after we've hit the sack.

CHAPTER 10

Corporate Sustainability Initiatives

This progress is all the more striking given that sustainability remains a modern preoccupation. This places new demands on business managers, who are under increasing pressure to foster long-term wealth rather than concentrate on the generation of short-term profit. Greater corporate concern for the environment provides an opportunity to shape new consumer markets. The future therefore looks increasingly attractive to those companies looking to sustainable products and lifestyles as major new business opportunities.

The move towards corporate sustainability has been remarkably buoyant over the past couple of years, with very little adverse effect from the current world financial crisis. This is a promising state of affairs; business has a central role to play in the transition to a more sustainable basis for society. Those companies working hard to tackle the challenge of sustainability have made encouraging progress to date. The application of innovation by companies to the realm of sustainability offers particularly good prospects for the future.

Carbon Offsetting and Emission Reduction Programs

A new concept, called a carbon reduction label, has hit Great Britain. The purpose of the label is to help consumers understand the carbon impact of the products and services they buy. This would help those who were interested in climate change when deciding where to spend their money. The Carbon Trust works with around 200 companies to measure the carbon impact of their products. This helps companies identify the "hotspots" in their operation and could help them reduce their carbon footprint, reduce costs, and improve their brand image. In the future, companies will follow a set of standards and use the carbon reduction label logo on their products and services as a certification for good corporate citizenship for the products they sell. This would allow consumers to understand the carbon impact of the specific product they are buying in parts of the supply chain. The goal of the program is simple: increase corporate carbon consciousness and contribute to the long-term success of the global campaign to combat climate change.

A new concept in environmental living is the idea of carbon offsets. A carbon offset is defined as reducing, avoiding or sequestering one metric ton of CO_2, or its equivalent, from being released into the Earth's atmosphere, according to the U.S. Environmental Protection Agency. What this means is that you can do something that causes greenhouse gases to be taken out of the air and buy it as a credit. For instance, do you drive a gas-hogging four-wheel-drive SUV and want to feel better about your gas consumption? A purchase of $50 will go to support such things like wind farms, methane gas capture from hog farms, energy from sun power, or reforestation in exchange for the purchase of a one-ton carbon offset. What would somebody get out of the deal? In essence, the purchase of a carbon offset means that you are doing something to help fund the fact that by-products of your vehicle are being taken out of our air.

CHAPTER 11

Government Policies and Regulations

But government vehicles alone, without the active help, support, and responsibility shown by each of us, by the businesses, organizations, and institutions, and by the countries and the international organizations, will most likely fail to make the needed difference. That is why you and I and thousands of others in whatever roles and at whatever levels we find ourselves must stridently and consistently exert the crucial "push" to ensure the success of practical green activities initially and green economic transformations ultimately.

Creating a sustainable future will be inconceivable without the active support of the local, national, and international governments. Governments play what is undoubtedly the most important role in this undertaking. Their economic, social, environmental, trade, and scientific policies, regulations, support systems, and incentives will pretty much determine what gets developed, to what extent in what period, by whom, and ultimately, how successfully.

Climate Change Agreements and Environmental Legislation

The following is a largely redundant, but generally up-to-date list of international climate change agreements and national or regional environmental legislation, presented only for context and reference purposes. A great many more agreements on biodiversity, desertification, and other environmental topics exist than are identified here. For purposes of equality, only one comprehensive uniform resource locator (URL) at a given level and for a given major topic has been selected, and that URL is often of a government agency closest to the topic and/or the location of the principal author of this site. The World Conservation Union (IUCN, in French) provides an excellent site for that organization (if interested). For regional overviews, many Regional Organizations provide data specific to their location. Also not presented herein are NGO-specific agglomerators, many principal environmental journals, and general environmental resources.

United Nations Framework Convention on Climate Change (UNFCCC)

Kyoto Protocol to the United Nations Framework Convention on Climate Change (UNFCCC)

North American Agreement on Environmental Cooperation (NAAEC)

History of the Statutory Basis for Current California Air Environmental Legislation

European Union's Climate Change Policies

Global Change Research Program at the U.S. Environmental Protection Agency

Global Change Research Supported by the National Aeronautics and Space Administration

CHAPTER 12

Educational Programs and Resources

Trade schools and vocational schools have additional programs that specifically cover green building technology, but there are too few of them. Eventually, all tradespeople and high school students involved with the building trade should experience multiple courses or school projects with green building technology. Colleges and universities have been actively creating four-year engineering and architecture programs that focus on green building. At some level, green building technology should be incorporated into the curricula of all engineering, design, and planning students, even if they are not specifically housed within an environmental department. Schools and colleges could benefit from greater coordination of complementary courses by offering specialization in other schools. Furthermore, community colleges and state universities can link with four-year colleges and establish shared programs with 2-year and 4-year college degree programs. Associations and business organizations offer programs ranging in length and topic. These programs educate those currently employed in the workforce setting on sustainable building.

Sustainable building educational programs are essential to creating progressive change in the building industry. It is important for all those currently employed in the business, including builders, architects, engineers, real estate professionals, subcontractors, and others, to gain a new appreciation, understanding, and enthusiasm for the benefits of green building. Educational programs in green building can take place on several levels, such as in high schools, vocational schools, trade schools, colleges, professional associations, and in the workplace.

Green Living Workshops and Online Platforms

As people become more aware of the need to protect the environment and use resources responsibly, there is a growing demand for services that promote sustainability. Green Living 2.0 is actively addressing this need by providing practical experiences and activities that inspire individuals and communities to embrace change. This chapter highlights various green living workshops and initiatives, which are organized through face-to-face interactions, online platforms, and green living certifications. The aim is to assist more groups in developing practical Education for Sustainability (EfS) programs that enhance knowledge and skills through a combination of reflection, dialogue, and action. By achieving this objective, the focus shifts from simply explaining why people should change to providing programs that demonstrate how to make meaningful adjustments in line with their values and concerns.

CHAPTER 13

Case Studies in Sustainable Living

It will be useful now to take a closer look at some specific case studies, to explore in some depth how people have successfully applied the principles of sustainable living in the real world economy. Again, what is presented here is but an introduction to an immense body of practical work that deserves much wider attention and adoption by people throughout the world. Combined with the broader strategies and purposes outlined in other sections of the Network's offering, there is indeed reason for much optimism about the prospect for a sustainable future.

Perhaps more than any single factor, demonstrating the viability and success of sustainability is essential to winning the hearts and minds of people around the globe. That's one function of the EcoNets service, and the many projects and strategies in the Network's purposes outlined in the previous chapters. Yet essential and inspiring as these projects and strategies are, they are but a beginning. Much more needs to be done, and on a much grander scale, if we are to create a global society where all people live in dignity, and do so within the means of the living, natural world.

Successful Green Communities

New communities developed by those who are consciously adopting greener technologies, but following western best practices have a lot to emulate. In addition, the majority of the material wealth in existing urbanized environments is created in richer homes and lifestyles typically produced less well-being than simpler lifestyles created in poor homes. Studies from metropolitan centers demonstrate that levels of active life and indeed happiness reached a maximum within limited wealth limits. Sustainable living is easier to refute if only community spirit is strong promoting physical fitness and mental stimulus are so much easier if people live physically close to the resources that keep them vibrant and growing. The concerns about sustainability are not only about a technique of finite carrying limits of life - what we use and what we throw away is as much about a critique of the societies we have become as anything else. By creating urban environments that satisfy the human need for community and physical fitness, we meet other human needs very effectively.

A green living approach is an opportunity to make a more radical change in our living environment by guiding the scientific and engineering technologies and detailed design. If coordinated approaches are adopted and rigorously adopted at a finer grain, then the efficacy of green changes that are made at the macro-regional level can be magnified. Both innovative design directions such as the ones we discussed earlier in the chapter act as good examples. The chapter dwells not just on high tech directions, but also on marginalized communities for which such changes have greater effect. Many academic studies assessed eco-cities, but these high tech cities represent a minority representation of new or existing cities. We all know that the greenest forms of human development are the simplest. It is extremely likely that the greenest communities over the centuries -

though not perhaps the most efficient - have been local poor and homely.

CHAPTER 14

Measuring and Tracking Sustainability Goals

This does not mean that we expect the family budget or the family environmental accounting statements to be audited by outside experts for their accuracy. There is nothing wrong with doing this sort of thing. Many people appreciate the value of financial planning and good financial management to their families and trust the work of accountants to tell them what they want to know about their financial performance. However, managing/verifying an environmental budget does not require the same level of managerial oversight and does not require the involvement of a CPA or the filing of a certified environmental report.

The importance of measuring and tracking progress toward a set of shared sustainability goals is not a new idea. In the business world, sustainability performance measures have been developing alongside financial performance measures for many years. When businesses fail to track progress, they find that the desired performance gains do not happen or lack of success is not understood until it is too late to do anything about it. The same is true for our society in general and for individual families. The sustainability goals that we have established, if they are to be taken seriously, deserve the same kind of careful tracking that we expect in the business world.

Key Performance Indicators and Metrics

The most important benchmark measurement is the one that precedes the sustainability improvement. Admittedly, this requires some fast footwork. But to quantify savings from improved equipment efficiency, it is only necessary to almost simultaneously collect operation and maintenance work order logs and utility bills. Preferred is the demand meter connected to a computer system to collect kilowatt (at 0.1-second intervals), temperature, cooling tower flow rate, chiller kWh, and other peak operational values. Preferable is to have last year's energy use on hand to develop the consumptive energy regression analysis model. Slightly reduced accuracy will result if such data is unavailable. However, the time relationships determined by this data can be followed and largely developed after energies are input in the benchmark software application program.

Specific weeks and periods are optimal for high-accuracy energy efficiency measurements. Prior to merely looking up the installations on the work order log, keeping a list of the locations will speed up, but not eliminate, data collection. However, it will save time onsite and facilitate the pre-planning so that once a task is initiated, it can be efficiently and effectively completed. Mobile technicians should be engaged to immediately fix water leaks, utility line breaks, and other significant waste streams that require immediate attention.

The foremost challenge associated with sustainability is that it is not always clearly discernible. Consider that newly implemented energy-efficient lighting has saved the company a substantial amount of money. The burning question is to what extent?

CHAPTER 15

The Future of Green Living

The emphasis on sustainable living as a moral imperative "hard-wired" into each generation is the essence of my book and the central hope of its conclusion: that the "normal" state of humankind will become harmony with the Earth, whether as a reaction to problems or as part of an ongoing evolution of human consciousness. Only then will every newly conceived human being inherit, practice, and pass down to the next generation not just guilt, fear, and judgment, but also a deep respect for the environment, an understanding of the many current interconnections between suffering people and our planet, a joy in positive actions that sustain the Earth, and a love of human generations yet to be.

I'm pleased that many governments at both the national and regional levels, influential organizations like the United Nations (UN), and even U.S.-based organizations have caught the green wave because only when we work together can we implement and enforce the policies, laws, and incentives necessary for green living. But laws and policies alone aren't enough. Real change happens at the individual level, with each and every home, office, community, city extending a hand in transforming existing structures or developing and building new ones. Mayors like New York City's Mike Bloomberg can affect great change, but so can individuals like you and me.

Innovations in Sustainable Technologies

This chapter uses innovations and initiatives to give you some concrete examples of how cutting-edge technology might be applied. While others are likely to think up and patent different technologies based on very similar principles in the same time frames, the examples are intended to provide you with an overview of how sustainability might be woven into all products. This is particularly addressed to those that will or should have the creation and design of next-generation technologies and products as their tasks. The examples in this chapter should give you a good impression of what kind of opportunities will present themselves and will also give you some ideas to explore with your engineering team about what sustainable design might mean in the context of two specific products you are developing.

Sustainability is fast becoming more than just an environmental catchphrase. Today, it is both possible and feasible to use cutting-edge technology to create the kinds of designs, systems, products, and services that will not only mitigate resource depletion, negative impacts on ecosystems and climate change, but also change the lives and revenues of the firms that choose to research, develop, and implement them. These technologies may also lay the groundwork for a next generation of products that increase in long-term value and that promote human and ecological health.

www.ingramcontent.com/pod-product-compliance
Lightning Source LLC
LaVergne TN
LVHW092100060526
838201LV00047B/1496